The Broad Highway

Reflections and Inspiration for Personal Transformation

Dr. Lennox G. Seales

AuthorHouse™ LLC
1663 Liberty Drive
Bloomington, IN 47403
www.authorhouse.com
Phone: 1-800-839-8640

Published by AuthorHouse 5/2/2014

ISBN: *978-1-4969-0196-5 (sc)*
          978-1-4969-0197-2 (e)

Library of Congress Control Number: 2014906101

authorHOUSE®

ACKNOWLEDGMENTS

I would like to thank my wife, Juanita, for her willingness and support of me in the publication of this book. Thanks to all of my teachers for their encouragement. Thanks to all of my clients who are forever challenging me to grow and expand spiritually. Love and hugs to my family of origin and extended family members for being a big part of everything that I do. To our children, Liane, Gabriel, and Vann; our daughter-in-law, Mara; and our grandson, Oliver. To Bernie Evans, who helped me with the initial editing. Love and blessings to all!

CONTENTS

INTRODUCTION

Thy word is a lamp for my feet, and a light unto my path.
—Psalm 119:105

I dwell in a deep sense of wonder. I believe in the mystery beyond all mysteries of thought, the world Florence Scovel Shinn refers to as "the world of the wondrous." I have experienced what it is like to be alive in this physical life, and it resonates with my inner being. Recovery for me is truly an inside job.

In this book of reflections, I am sharing thoughts and experiences that I find beneficial in helping me to face pain, to face the need to change self-defeating behaviors, to help me forgive myself again and again, and to grow and to become the person that God intended me to be in this physical life. We learn that the realm of the spirit is broad and roomy. My hope for those reading this book is that they will take what they need and leave the rest. I am quite sure that everything here won't necessarily be of interest to you in your life process. But all in all, I hope that by sharing, I will aid someone in his or her process of growth and healing.

In the end, life is a do-it-yourself project. So take it nice and slow, and sample my offerings, just for today.

To see a world in a grain of sand
And a heaven in a wild flower,
Hold infinity in the palm of your hand
And eternity in an hour
—William Blake

SPIRITUAL GROWTH THROUGH THE BLUES

*Finally, brethren, whatsoever things are true, whatsoever things
are honest, whatsoever things are just, whatsoever things are pure,
whatsoever things are lovely, whatsoever things are of good report, if
there be any virtue, and if there be any praise, think on these things.*

—Philippians 4:8

So many of us live our lives preoccupied with our problems. We are stressed, broken-down, overwhelmed, and in need of an overhaul. We walk around feeling less than sufficient. The challenges of life and our willingness to disconnect in the twenty-first century make us vulnerable, powerless, and impotent. Truth be known, focusing on our problems allows them to expand and leaves us more deeply disconnected. The blues can be an agent that serves us by distracting our mind.

Get outside of your head and connect to a shot of Big Mama Thornton's "Sweet Little Angel." It is guaranteed to set you right. It will expand your imagination, transcend your limits, and give you the ability to see yourself as boundless and connected to light. We limit ourselves when we become isolated in our heads. Try on some of Ray Charles's "Let's Have a Ball." The blues is a vehicle that releases us and provides opportunities for creative voices to manifest. Praying the blues is the ability to take action and find a way out of any kind of stuck place.

Avail yourself of Pat Martino's passionate playing on Monk's "Round Midnight." Blues power can be a catalyst to finding connection and value in life. Martino speaks the language of the soul with his guitar. He has the ability to engage you on a level that is most uncommon. It is safe to say that many look for and settle for the ordinary; consequently, they will miss his music. It is the music that takes you inward toward self and helps you clean up the rubbish that keeps you blocked.

Pat Martino is the Picasso of the jazz guitar today. Everyone who listens carefully to his playing will eventually realize that he is, in my estimation, connected to higher energy fields. He jumps out and gracefully paints notes on the canvas of hearts and minds, producing warm and powerful feelings that affect my being. I get a new exhilaration of mind, with a greater and greater desire to move toward the spiritual side of myself. His truth flows out through his notes to manifest new love in me to know and have more as I fall into harmony with my higher self.

I will leave the negatives without fear. I will move into a pure imaginative state of well-being. There is a special place where I am able to release the burdens and jump out of my body. The material loads are lifted, and I no longer feel miserable; I am in a process of growth.

Be willing to turn yourself and your thoughts away from the ordinary toward the spiritual, so you can dwell on your good and the good in others; then all of the toxic energy will leave you. Practice listening and releasing. Following Paul's advice to the Philippians at the start of this lesson, we can learn to turn away from the mind of flesh and move toward the mind of spirit.

DIVINE MESSAGES

*For thine is the kingdom and the power
and the glory, forever, amen.*

—Matthew 6:13

Every day in every way, we are surrounded by divine messages. Never underestimate the source of these messages. Take time today to reflect and to meditate on the above portion of the Lord's Prayer. If you think and believe that you are not enough for the glory, my guess is you won't manifest power or glory in this physical life. However, if you believe that you are and you ask for it, you will connect with the power that is available to each of us.

Turn on the switch and watch what happens. We will live life with a positive expectancy. We are prepared to have more of what we ask for. We expand, and gradually we find the path to our own authentic selves. Once we claim our authentic selves and follow that path, we will find that, bit by bit, little by little, things will fall into place. The relationship, the money, the home, and the friends will come together if that is what we want.

*Man goes through many births and deaths, until he knows the truth
which sets him free. … Man's freedom comes through fulfilling his
destiny, bringing into manifestation the Divine Design of his life.*

—Florence Scovel Shinn

DIVINE PATTERNS

But seek ye first the kingdom of God, and his righteousness;
and all these things shall be added unto you.

—Matthew 6:33

There is a divine pattern for each life. However, we would hardly be able to discover what it is without availing ourselves of the right ideas. Right ideas come from God. I believe that we are here in this life to do things no one else can do for us.

There is a perfect plan for every life. We sometimes see a flash of it, and sometimes we are intimidated and alone. Becoming fearful of the gifts given us, we self-destruct. We take a detour, and we strive for things that do not belong, things that can only result in failure and regret. We are locked into the ego; we are alone, living in the bondage of self-centered fear. We live the most difficult lives in the disconnected state.

We must find the courage to live a creative authentic life. It truly does not matter what we find to do creatively. It is going to be a lot less difficult than living in the disconnect.

THE BROAD HIGHWAY OF LIFE

Therefore I say unto you, what things so ever ye desire,
when ye pray, believe that ye receive them,
and ye shall have them.

—Mark 11:24

Yes, today is a good day to get on the broad highway of life. Are you dreaming dreams and feeling like they are impossible to achieve? Instead of feeling overwhelmed, find a new way to see yourself accomplishing those dreams.

Never place limitations on yourself; expand your limits. Don't just survive, thrive. Get rolling on the broad highway and drive forward. Find a way to attach to infinite possibilities. Know that God has already taken account for us. We are already in his family.

The Lord is my shepherd; I shall not want.

—Psalm 23:1

STEP BY STEP

Keep thy heart (imagination) with all diligence,
for out of it are the issues of life.

—Proverb 4:23

Step by step, we move along. Sometimes we step into a dark and discouraging place. Many of us just quit trying. We give up and lose hope, becoming overwhelmed and discouraged. Could it be we started out with an image or a belief that we were not good enough, or a conflicted attitude? These images and beliefs manifest themselves in our lives.

I have seen many people fall into this puddle, only to give up doing the next right thing. Get quiet and refocus your sights. Get out of your own way and get rid of the sticky stuff. Do not attach yourself to permanence. Many of life's circumstances are fleeting. Put some Teflon on your thoughts and become unstuck.

It was in Napoleon Hill's publication of his philosophy of personal achievement, *Think and Grow Rich*, where I stumbled onto the message, "Whatever the mind can conceive and believe, it can achieve." This captured my imagination. It sincerely took me into that self-actualizing place. Put your energy on all that you believe is possible today. Do not allow anyone to tell you what to think or do or be. Detach from your family limits, your cultural limits, your educational limits, or any other limits imposed upon you. You do not have to live up to anyone's story or expectation. Do not look back, or you are going to crash. Look to today.

It was Jesus who said, "No man having put his hand to the plow and looking back is fit for the kingdom of heaven" (Luke 9:62). Keep on detaching and use your powerful imagination. You are going to become a powerful receptor of ideas, thoughts, and knowledge that will take you beyond all limits. Your authentic powers are going to help you to live your dreams. It is the reason that you manifest your dreams in the first place.

We are only willing to discount our dreams when we see them as coming from a lower place. We are much more equipped to act on our dreams when we realize that God almighty has placed them into our minds and hearts. Don't panic! You were selected to manifest greatness. Embrace those dreams and allow them to take root deep down in your inner being.

Remember that fear and doubts are coming from your limited self. Fear and doubts will never come from Almighty God. Align yourself with he who has all power and knowledge. You are here to live your life; please do not allow any compromise to take hold of you and take you to defeat. God will allow you to manifest those dreams if you are willing to do your portion of the work.

As a teenager, I saw James Brown on the *Mike Douglas Show*. Mike Douglas referred to him as, "James Brown, the hardest-working man in show business." James took a seat on the panel. Mike Douglas said, "James, to what do you owe your success?"

James responded, "Success is 10 percent inspiration and 90 percent perspiration."

I learned a great lesson that day from James Brown. Nothing takes the place of hard work and persistence. Talent alone is not enough to insure success. I have met lots of talented people who failed miserably. I remember one friend who told me to be resilient and to be determined and the rest will take care of itself. Could it be that God takes care of the rest when we demonstrate willingness and honesty to believe and do our work?

It takes time to arrive at any good place in this life. It is about the waiting game. There is an art to waiting, and almost none of us likes to wait. Wait anyway. Waiting is high art. It will definitely take time to master the art of waiting. Learn to lock into your dreams and ideas. Perseverance means locking into your ideas and rocking steadily forward. You will eventually roll down the highway of success.

I remember when I was younger and living in a Brooklyn tenement. We had a hot-water faucet in the bathroom that had a steady drip. It was the bathtub faucet. Those tubs were covered in heavy thick porcelain, but eventually that drip penetrated the porcelain and the entire spot became black from the drip wearing the porcelain away. I learned a lesson on the power of persistence.

If we are willing to continue the journey into our authentic selves, the potency of persistence and perseverance will take us right on to a flood of goodness and success.

THE POWER OF CONNECTION

Isolation hardly works to help us to grow and serve. This is an Adlerian concept referred to as *gemeinschaftsgefuhl*. The term refers to an individual's attitude in dealing with the social world, and it includes striving for a better future for humans.

Psychologist Alfred Adler believed that social interest and a sense of empathy and identification with others was of the utmost importance to help us promote personal goals that guide behavior. "When we are able to see with the eyes of another, to hear with the ears of another, to feel with the heart of another, we are truly in connection with that person." One of the most important aspects of Adler's individual psychology rests on the belief that our happiness and success are largely related to our social connectedness. Stay connected!

LESSON #8

PRIVATE LOGIC

I have listened to many people who are forever spilling their private logic concerning their position in life or their situations. Psychologist Alfred Adler coined the term *private logic* to refer to the concept of self, others, and life that constituted the philosophy on which an individual's life is based.

More often than not, our problems are based on our conclusions, our private logic, which do not conform to the reality of social living. Most of what will hold us back are faulty assumptions and conclusions. We must discover our basic mistakes and learn how to correct these assumptions. We could be selling ourselves a bill of goods that will forever keep us off of the broad highway of life.

Some of us walk around believing that no one could care for us, or we are too quick to reject others before they have a chance to reject us. We are always invested in perfection and ignoring progress. We believe and behave as if things will never work out well. We play God and we remain inflexible, embracing what we perceive as a state of permanence. We are the first to act surprised when we experience failure. We travel with enormous guilt and toxic shame, since we forever believe that we are letting everyone down.

Quit! Find the courage to change these faulty assumptions and see your way to the broad highway of life. Embrace impermanence and open-mindedness. Life is fluid, not rigid and inflexible. Do not be a prisoner of your thoughts and lock yourself up into a life of lack and limitations. There is an energy that is available wherever and whenever you are ready.

THE FLOW

Life throws you lemons and you embrace them, hoping that by crying out, you will change your circumstances. Don't beat yourself up today. It's never the circumstances that define us—it is more about our disposition.

The worst of times are temporary. Take a long nap and see what that does for you in trying times. Some people will say, "I cannot sleep when things are difficult." Change that belief, knowing that when things are rough, you already lack the power to fix the problem on your own. Napping is a way of regrouping and giving you an opportunity to replenish energy.

No need to fall apart when you are dealing with life's difficulties. It does not help to berate and tear yourself apart. Have mercy and know that you need to find your way to the flow rather than get stuck in situations.

We are never far from the flow of life. It is more our belief that we are far that sets us apart. Get into the flow of life and quit thinking. Find the flow, a path of pure simplicity that allows you to be easy on yourself. Don't be hard on yourself; it won't help anyone. No one will benefit from your negativity. There is enough ugliness in the world, and therefore no need to pass it on.

End the torment and refuse to share torment. Avoid serving your pain up to others. Expand by finding the simple pleasures of joy, willingness, self-honesty, and humility. Most of all, answer these questions: Do you believe that intellect is enough to solve all of your problems?

If you realize that it is not, then get busy and start expanding toward your higher power source.

It was only a matter of being willing to believe in a power greater than myself. Nothing more was required of me to make my beginning.

—*The Big Book of Alcoholics Anonymous*, page 12, line 18

THE POWER OF MUSIC

He restoreth my soul.

—Psalm 23:3

Different experiences will help us to feel restored, like the feelings that come from restful sleep, good food, listening to music, or enjoying a live performance by your favorite player or performer. Somehow, the marriage of great ideas and the combination of body and soul will take us to a restoration of the soul. It is when we become one with God.

It appears that when we are one with God, wonderful gifts and ideas come to visit us. God gives us the power to create things and to do things with our bodies and minds. Music is something that I use to restore my soul. I often listen to the music of Pat Martino. Martino's playing has restorative powers, and its impact on me is profound.

Lately, when I drive my grandson Oliver to school, I have seen that the music has a wonderful impact on him as well. He gets quiet, and he goes into some special place when the music is playing. He is no longer restless and miserable in his seat. He has this serene look on his face that is very different for him. I always make sure that I play Martino whenever he is in the car. It appears that the music influences his thoughts, and consequently he sits back and calms down, as if he truly understands the power of this music.

OCTOBER

I let go of September knowing that summer is gone. Labor Day is behind us, and I am ready for the transition into cooler nights and soup cooking in the kitchen. Leaves are moving and flying around, with new colors everywhere. Festivals, country fairs, and pies are coming into being. Halloween and making believe are around the corner. Fall is in the air.

Find meaning in your life and get to work. Find the pleasurable things that offer you value and therapy. We must find healing and inspiration in life, in our family life and in our friends and our community. Stay locked into goodness and avoid any pull toward isolation.

MAINTAINING

Find that steady groove and keep it going. It takes practice and willingness to keep the wheels turning well. We can change our entire attitude about maintaining our bodies, friendships, relationships, families, homes, cars, toys, tools, instruments, and life. Nice and easy still does it better that ripping and running around.

Most of us are busy striving and never arrive at that place where there is authentic love. We find hollow loneliness and excess baggage that bloats us more and more. We have the power to change ourselves in order to meet the unforeseen.

Take your time, do the vigorous painstaking work, and discover the defects that drive you into serious and deadly emotional disaster. Have mercy on yourself today. Be that person you respect, and create a willing attitude in which to nurture and become more authentic.

I was walking in the Publix parking lot in Pooler recently when I saw a car coming at me at a very high rate of speed. I happened to be in the pedestrian crosswalk at the time, and this driver completely ignored me. I stepped back and said to myself, *Gosh, she is in a mighty big hurry*. Suddenly I heard a car horn blowing and a bang coming from ahead of where I was. Someone had pulled out of a parking space and hit this woman broadside. I wondered, *God, what was that about?*

WHY AM I HERE?

The wailing of broken hearts is the doorway to God.

—Rumi, "The Agony of Lovers"

Answer the question, "Why am I here?" Find your passion, and you are going to experience a harmony and a sense of knowingness. You will be in tune with the reason you are here. Whatever brought you to this life is sufficient, and it is going to show you what you are here to do. You will soon find that you are able to serve God and help mankind.

Stay connected to that still small voice that you hear all the time. Do not turn your back on that voice, or else you will move into the disconnected. Moreover, fear will come, and you will face unnecessary pain if you ignore that voice. Move closer toward what you already know. The best part about moving closer is that it takes you further, beyond the point where you are now.

You are not going to fail. You are enough, and you have everything it takes to be successful. Stop embracing the illusion of failure. Life gives us feedback each time we attempt anything. Stop the judgment, and keep on availing yourself of the opportunity to continue the process of doing and serving others. Each time you attempt, you are getting better.

Be mindful that there is always that voice of judgment hanging around to discourage you. It is what it is, and it takes what it takes, so it is about your process of growing and being in the world. The object is to become more and more yourself, so how could it be wrong? The passion that you feel is coming from deep within you. Serve others today and disconnect from the serving yourself.

TURNING TO THE FATHER OF LIGHT

It meant destruction of self-centeredness.
I must turn in all things to the Father of Light who presides over us all.

—*The Big Book of Alcoholics Anonymous, page 14*

Some days I want to believe that the entire world revolves around me and what I want, but it is simply not true. My attitudes and my behaviors are coming from deep down inside me. I recognize when I am coming in from childhood. The experiences of childhood formed my perception of me and many of my life's mistakes.

I recognize my unfinished business. I see my painful past that I continue to work through. I carry parts of the past deep down within me. I stop and reflect every time I am caught up in my personal travails. I have to pray for deliverance and healing to take place in those parts of me. I know that in the end, I will grow through those experiences, knowing that they are lessons that I have to master as I walk my way home.

Today, I have to get over my past. If I am still struggling with my childhood or any experience that I perceive as toxic, I truly embrace what Bill W. suggested. That is, if we want to reduce self-centeredness, we must turn to the Father of Light for help. It appears that we are seldom able to reduce our self-centeredness much by ourselves. We must recognize and accept powerlessness in order to move toward a higher power. If we insist on using the mind that gets us into trouble to get us out of trouble, we are lost indeed.

THE MOON BELONGS TO EVERYONE EVERYWHERE

That ye may be the children of your Father which is in heaven: for he maketh his sun to rise on the evil and on the good and sended rain on the just and on the unjust.

—Matthew 5:45

It is a wonderful truth for me to realize that the moon is there for everyone who wants to take time to reflect on its majesty. Sit quietly and analyze this truth. There is no denying anyone or discrimination against anyone when it comes to the moon. It does not matter who you are, where in the world you are, your class, your race, your religion, your status, your sexual orientation, your profession, your political affiliation, the moon is there for all of us.

The moon does not show preference to any group. We are all included in the light and the power of the moon. So we are all covered and included under heaven, as mentioned in the passage from Matthew above.

LESSON #16

THE FOUR HORSEMEN

Let not your heart be troubled,

neither be afraid.

—John 14:27

You must admit that there are days when you are overcome by thoughts of unworthiness. No matter how much you fight those nagging feelings, they seem to creep into your consciousness and pronounce you a failure. Time after time, these four horsemen that are written about in the Big Book—terror, bewilderment, frustration, and despair—come to drag you away to the scrapheap of society.

Have you had these feelings that no matter what you do, you are incapable? That no matter what, you cannot be fixed, and you won't be cured? Yes, you have had a sense of what I am referring to; you could safely say that you have experienced a sense of powerlessness.

Feeling powerless is truly part of living life. Powerlessness is a pain that we experience in this life. No matter who you are, I could generalize the belief that in this physical life, we all experience some form of powerlessness. In some ways, we have all been driven by our powerlessness. The pain of powerlessness is real.

Oftentimes we are reaching out deep into the world, trying to find something to hang on to that will relieve us of our pain and hopefully give us some sense of power. It may be a person, it may be a place or a position, it may be acquiring things like a car, a home, jewelry, money in the bank, or investments. It could be drugs or sex. It is false to believe that we are going to find any such thing to make us worthy, safer, or comfortable in our skin.

Striving for these external sources of power is endless. No one truly finds that power outside of self. Powerlessness serves to distract us and manipulates us, taking

23

us to hospitals, prisons, treatment centers, holy men and women, unemployment, underemployment, and the undertaker. The Big Book says, "It was only a matter of being willing to believe in a power greater than myself. Nothing more was required of me to make my beginning."

Many of us have found a new beginning and a new meaning in our existence, and it is all because we came to believe in a power greater than ourselves. Today, I simply call this power my God. I saw that I could live my life on a new foundation; I could be the person that I was intended to be without any reservation or strife. I am willing to believe and flow freely down the stream of life.

I remember my father once saying to me, "Son, promise me that you are going to live your own life." It was a great realization, coming to terms with the obvious idea that I had a life of my own to live, to truly be me. Dad was not only encouraging, he was giving me permission. Despite this knowledge, we are still caught up daily in seeking external power. We must strive to stay aligned with the one power that will help relieve our powerlessness. We have to do the daily work of praying, reflecting, behaving, and asking for strength and direction to do the right things to heal our powerlessness.

Continue to believe daily in your higher power. He will relieve you based on your willingness to demonstrate belief. He will relieve you based on the level of your belief. There will be no social promotions or wishful thinking. Give up the magic and go and do the daily work. If you are currently in recovery, continue to attend recovery meetings and make yourself do the work that needs to be done. Listen to the experiences of others who are successful. Do not be quick to judge old-timers in the program. Make sure to find something that you need for your journey.

I have seen too many people walk away from their recovery-group meetings with the false belief that they are sober and have things under control. The decision to walk away is another one of those false agreements we make with ourselves. It does not take long before you are slipping in some vital area of your life. You may not always pick up a drug or a drink at first. Powerlessness will manifest itself in a multiplicity of ways. Stay vital, stay invested, stay connected, and never take anything for granted; this is the great shift.

The shift is about staying connected to a community of health and wholeness, learning to resist the impulse to act out emotionally and do familiar things. We must do the opposite of what we have done. Practice doing the opposite behaviors and the new self will eventually emerge. We create authentic energies that flow into us and flow through us. We no longer go out to look for the good; we go in to be real and whole.

One must practice doing the opposite behavior over and over. We are going to know authentic power for the first time when we do. We will no longer feel empty, faulty, and fearful. We will be connected, and we will feel wholesome.

Change yourself with love and make the decision to give up the agreements that define your life and cement your powerlessness. We learn finally to give up faulty beliefs and behaviors for healthy agreements. We are going to slowly create and move into the authentic powers of man. To have more and to be more is the way of truth. Slowly, we will come back.

MY SEASON OF WILLINGNESS

God is our refuge and strength,
a very present help in trouble.

—Psalm 46:1

I allow myself to feel good every day about something. Stop bathing your brain in negative thoughts. I encounter darkness, emptiness, prejudice, delusions, pain, denial, greed, and all of the things that serve to lock us up in our egos, hurts, hatred, and strife; we are then limited as we travel through this life.

Now I see clearly that when I am overwhelmed, afraid, and bathing my brain in my powerlessness, all I need to do to replenish my supply is to stop and do my daily rituals. It's about opposites: seeing a mighty God rather than a powerless self. I allow myself to reflect on him who has all power, who has all knowledge, who is able to do exceedingly abundantly above all that I ask or think, according to the power that works in me.

THE SILENCE

A double-minded man is unstable in all his ways.

—James 1:8

There is much joy and sadness every day in the world. There are times when I encounter sadness and pain and no joy. I allow the experience to create an impression in me that takes me to discouragement. I behave as if I have a guarantee of never having pain or sadness again.

I know now that pain is unavoidable. The creative enlightened person learns to see pain and sadness in a different way. I know that I am caught many times in my discouragement, and it takes me to powerlessness. I question God, but not for long. I soon get redirected to the answers when I go to the silence again.

In the place Nelson Mandela refers to as "the silence," the answer is never about not having pain or sadness. It is about working through these issues and letting them go their way as fast as possible. I let go, and I let God do for me what I find impossible to do for myself. So it is never about changing my mind or avoiding the difficulties of life.

Learning to face pain and working through pain is where the joy is. Could it be then that joy and pain are the two sides of the same coin? Accepting this truth helps me to stay in the moment and avoid looking and staying in the past. Take what you need and leave the rest. Come to terms with your life the way that it is today, with lots of joy and lots of pain.

In the Big Book, page 85, line 5, Bill Wilson writes, "We are not fighting it, neither are we avoiding temptation. We feel as though we had been placed in a position of neutrality—safe and protected." Understand the spiritual ways of being.

Happy is the man that findeth wisdom,

And the man that getteth understanding.

For the gaining of it is better than the gaining of silver,

And the profit thereof than fine gold.

She is more precious than rubies:

And none of the things thou canst desire are to be compared unto her.

Length of days is in her right hand;

In her left hand are riches and honor.

Her ways are ways of pleasantness,

And all her paths are peace.

She is a tree of life to them that lay hold upon her:

And happy is every one that retained her.

With all thy getting get understanding.

—Proverbs 3:13–18

THE GREAT REALITY

—Proverbs 3:13–18, 4:7

True understanding is the realization that intellect is not enough. Acquiring knowledge does not guarantee peace. As Bill Wilson wrote on page 55 of the Big Book, line 19: "We found the Great Reality deep down within us. In the last analysis it is only there that He may be found."

Man acquires intellectual perceptions of truth. Real truth has to be revealed to the consciousness of a person. The revelation of real truth is the beginning of understanding the spiritual path. "And Jesus answered and said unto him, Blessed are thou, Simon Bar-jo'na: for flesh and blood had not revealed it unto thee, but my Father which is in heaven" (Matthew 16:17).

Knowing self has more to do with the understanding and the consciousness that deep down in the depths of your being is a place where you connect to the Father. All health, all wisdom, all joy is already in your being, ready to jump out at you as you call or need. The consciousness of this truth is the beginning of spiritual understanding. Coming into oneness with the Father is absolutely required of all of us who have decided to seek self.

The journey from our heads to our hearts is the one we must take. Jesus's plan is to join us in the external, because that is where we live. We must travel inward to the father of light who presides over all of us so that we may find oneness with him.

Detaching From Dysfunction

As far as the east is from the west,
so far hath he removed our transgressions from us.

—Psalm 103:12

Often we are not aware that it is difficult to stop carrying unnecessary pain and other dysfunctional relationships, experiences, and situations. Over and over, I meet with folks who appear to be so content to repeat the same toxic experiences and encounters, as if by telling the same story one more time with passion they will change the experience. It is evident that all of it comes from a powerless place, and no amount of passion will make things better or change the way things are.

Winning by losing is a very uncommon concept. However, detaching doesn't mean that you are losing; it is more about changing the way you see and respond to things in order to make a change. Change can happen, and when it does you feel better. Change does not always have to be profound; it could be subtle as well.

We experience the energy of God when we are ready. I recognize this energy, and I know it is not to be reflected on as much as it is to be experienced. I stay conscious that a higher power resides in me today and always. It is the consciousness of my own personal God that takes me out of darkness into the light. I get quiet, I allow myself to be submerged into this inner energy, and I bathe my mind in this energy. Practice bathing your mind in this inner light and watch what happens.

Be still, and know that I am God.

—Psalm 46:10

30

KEEPING AN OPEN MIND TO RECEIVE

Today I will stay open-minded to receive what is good. I know now that my limits and my lack in life are more about counting my problems than my blessings. I am sometimes blind to the things that life is giving me and receptive to what I perceive it is not. However, I also realize that whenever I tune my mind toward being receptive to goodness, I transcend these blocks.

There are times when I encounter my worthlessness, and my energy supply gets low. I feel like I do not deserve to have the good things in life. My vision is blocked, and I vibrate very low. I cannot see things working in my best interest. Helping others and being of service to others has always moved me away from that place of falsehood and selfishness. I am able to see abundance again; it becomes clear that the more I help others, the more I help myself. I recognize my ability, and I am grateful that I have found my missing piece that keeps me glued together.

I have worked with many people whose intentions are to take and never give. I ask God to put a hedge around me. I have known those who have taken, not realizing that I am aware the behavior. I know that the universe has a perfect accounting system. We will all pay—no one gets out without paying for everything that was taken that does not belong to the taker. This is the law of karma. It is what the Sanskrit refers to as "comeback."

Let us draw near with true heart in full assurance of faith, having our hearts sprinkled from evil conscience, and our bodies washed with pure water. Let us hold fast the profession of our faith without wavering; (for the faithful that promised;).

—Hebrews 10–22, 23

GROWING UP

When I was a child, I spoke as a child; I understood as a child,
I thought as a child: but when I became a man,
I put away childish things.

—1 Corinthians 13:11

Coming to terms with the part of maturity that has to do with acceptance is crucial. I've realized that lot of what I wanted all of my life does not manifest just because I am older. Also, it becomes very apparent that many needs that I have had are no good for me today—needs that I carried from childhood and those I attached myself to all of my life may no longer serve me well.

Look at your needs and determine what is healthy and what is important and good for you now. Attending to your own needs and becoming aware of them is totally dependent on you and no one else. Do not develop relationships hoping that another person will take care of your needs. Become accountable to yourself first.

THE POWER OF DESIRE

My words shall not return unto me void,
but shall accomplish that where unto it is sent.

—*Isaiah 55:11*

More and more, I've come to believe that desire is a very powerful force operating within me. It is my understanding that desire has to be directed into the right areas of life or else it results in catastrophic chaos. Pay attention to where your desires are directed. Play the tape all the way and make sure you do the research as to all consequences that could result.

Do your desires serve you only? Chances are, if they serve only you, you should make a decision to redirect them to serve and to help others. Pay attention to your words. Know that your words and thoughts are capable of transmitting powerful vibrations that will manifest in your body and in your affairs.

Say this prayer: "God, Reveal to me my assignment for today. Let me go and be of service to someone who could benefit from my being there. I ask this in Jesus's holy name today. Amen."

Only I discern infinite passion,
and the pain of finite hearts that yearn.

—*Robert Browning*

FINDING MY RECEPTIVE STATE

All things are possible.

—Matthew 19:26

Today in my receptive state, I am worthy of receiving my good. I am aware of my blocks, and I harness the force of attraction so that I avoid attracting my blocks. I am happy and healthy to receive, and I trust the universe to deliver goodness to me all the day long without question.

I detach with love from my negativity, knowing that my negativity is coming from my limited self. The mind of flesh wants to dictate and project limits onto me. My nature is striving and always wanting to produce goodness so that my needs are met. All of my limited thinking is taking place in my unconscious mind. I will, one day at a time, counter the intentions of my limited self.

KEEP ON EXPANDING

According to your faith be it done unto you.

—*Matthew 9:29*

It is never enough to just be sober. Being sober is the beginning of a wonderful new life, if you are willing to let go and do the daily work. The operative word here is *work*. Yes, not magic or wishful thinking, just willingness to face pain and work daily. We must be willing to grow, to expand, and to give up old ways of thinking and being, to be willing to do the opposite of everything we have done in the past that brought us to the place where we are right now.

So often I see newly sober people who show up with a head full of ideas as to what they need to do, or not wanting to do what is suggested. They tell me how much they are going to do and all sorts of faulty beliefs and assumptions that keep them yardbirds forever. Sadly, these people will eventually go out and relapse again and again, missing the point every time and never learning to fly.

One of the problems is that they miss the understanding of being in a conversion process. They miss the purpose of becoming transformed. They come into recovery remaining stuck in their self-directed life. They talk about what they don't want to do because they keep themselves on the throne. They lock the higher power outside of their lives, and they proceed to be directed by self, which more often than not results in more misery confusion and the police, because nothing changes.

The first step of Alcoholics Anonymous states that, "We admitted we were powerless over alcohol—that our lives had become unmanageable." If we truly admit powerlessness, then it stands to reason that power must come from the one who is still on the throne.

The second step states that we "came to believe that a Power greater than ourselves could restore us to sanity." The implication here is that the self is willing to yield to a higher power. One must first try to realize that he lacks the power to make himself be restored to his sound mind, and therefore he is yielding to a higher power source to provide that will.

The third step states that we "made a decision to turn our will and our lives over to the care of God *as we understood Him*." We made a decision after we tried it on our own, and it is clear by the evidence shown that we have failed to do the job. Now we are willing to get help. We have lived life our own way, and we are now willing to live it God's way. We are no longer interested in directing our lives. We are seeking God's direction.

I truly believe that it is time we firm this idea up for folks so that they are able to fully come to terms with the issue of powerlessness over addicted substances. If we are truly sincere, we are going to benefit in our recovery as a result of being in harmony with God's plan for us. God's plan is the plan that takes us from darkness to light and from death to life. Recovery is truly transformational. In recovery, we become the authentic people that God intended us to become. Recovery is a conversion experience.

Wherefore, my beloved, as ye have always obeyed,
not as in my presence only, but now much more in my absence,
work out your own salvation with fear and trembling.
For it is God which worketh in you both
to will and to do of his good pleasure.

—Philippians 1:12–13

OWN WAY CHILD

I remember growing up in the Caribbean. I can still recall hearing many parents refer to a child as an "own way child." It meant that the child was defiant or unruly in some way. Truth be known, it was never good to hear a mother refer to her child as "own way." It stuck in my mind that "own way" children were headed for trouble. I would silently promise myself never to be "own way." I had bad visions coming into my mind as to what would happen if I were to be "own way."

Today in my work, I meet many young men and women who lead a very self-directed life—essentially, a life wherein they serve only themselves. Often, the result is a life that is unmanageable, one that involves mood-altering substances, the criminal-justice system, school failure, destructive relationships, and loss of family support. In most cases, it is plain to see that these young people have stumbled into darkness, and many are lost in a life of regret.

What is the real meaning of these losses and regrets? I ask myself, could it be that as children and young people, we separate ourselves from parental guidance, but more importantly, we became separated from God's love? Many times over, we go the way of a self-directed lifestyle rather than a Christ-directed life.

It is important to note that most twelve-step programs advocate a return to God as a means of being restored. On pages 70–71 of the Big Book, Bill Wilson writes:

> In this book you read again and again that faith did for us what we could not do for ourselves. We hope you are convinced now that God can remove whatever self-will has blocked you off from Him. If you have already made a decision, and an inventory of your grosser handicaps, you have made a good beginning. That being so you have swallowed and digested some big chunks of truth about yourself.

Essentially, restoration is about a return to God as we understand God. It is about turning to him when we are truly ready to quit doing and living by our own devices. Wilson reinforces the idea that help comes from a belief in God on page 164 of the Big Book, where he writes, "Abandon yourself to God as you understand God. Admit your faults to Him and to your fellows. Clear away the wreckage of your past. Give freely of what you find and join us. We shall be with you in the Fellowship of the Spirit, and you will surely meet some of us as you trudge the Road of Happy Destiny. May God bless you and keep you until then."

MEDITATIONS AND DAILY REFLECTIONS
FOR CLARITY AND CHANGE

Coming In from the Storm

Every day in every way, God is bringing me out of the storm again and again.

I know I am shining bright tonight. His wonderful glory and honor sustain me.

Night and day through the storm I roll on through, and I sing wonderful praises to him who has all power to move mountains and the rivers. I know and I believe that he is bringing me out of the storms again and again.

Dance with the Wind

Dance with the winds of change.

Dance in oneness; keep the rhythm steady and never drop the beat again.

Find the sameness and move away from the differences.

Dance away stagnation and get hold of growth.

Dance all night and all day, like you really want to dance the day away.

Dance from bondage and unnecessary pain;

act like your life depends on it, again and again.

Dance your way to freedom, dance out of bondage,

so you know the difference between the two.

Into the Water

Don't ask me why.

I am into the water. I am withholding nothing.

God, I want you to wash away all of my pain for today. I am willing to give you all that I am carrying, because I am weary and in need of your energy. I am powerless, and I am weary and in need of your love. My drinking and my drugging let me down. I am beat up, locked up, and I still can't stop.

My mama done left me, my daddy too; my sisters and brothers don't want anything to do with me anymore. My so-called friends are nowhere to been found, and the judge, he told me he or the undertaker going to put me away for good. Lord, I am into the water, so could you wash me clean?

I am willing to let you be my master and my higher power.

Shaking Unnecessary Pain

Shake gently and steady all the way; sometimes you have to shake it down all day.

Shake down all the negatives that are coming at you.

Shake it once, shake it twice, it gets better when you shake it nice.

No one going to shake for you; it's your monkey that's up your tree. You may have to twist and turn yourself around, but go ahead and keep on shaking that monkey to the ground.

Rainbow

I heard a woman say that when things grow grey

and your life is filled with nothing but despair,

don't give up and walk away.

Look again, and you will see a rainbow for you to hang on to.

There is always a rainbow.

Slow down and embrace your fears.

There is a rainbow; settle down, and you will get past despair.

Listen to the whisper.

There is always hope.

Look, over yonder, there is a rainbow coming for you and for me today.

I Thank You for Saving Me

Every day in every way

I need your love

to help me out.

I took a lot for granted,

and I went astray,

but I saw the light at the crossroads and found my way.

Every day in every way I am thankful for the love you gave.

Lord, I am grateful for your love.

Lord, I am thankful to you for saving me.

Fire Within

I feel the fire within me—

I feel it down deep.

I feel the fire within me—

from my head to my toes.

As my mother lie dying,

I realize how little is left for me to do;

I am powerless over death.

I am bewildered, and I know

I am trying to hold on

'cause in less than a day

my mama will be gone.

I feel the fire within me—

it burns brighter by the hour.

It's been a long time since that night.

I still feel the fire; it will never ever burn out.

Heaven Room

I love to sit in my heaven room,

catch some rays and a little groove.

I like to wish the world away.

I make believe I am not here

in my heaven room.

We could wish away the cares

in my heaven room as

hours turn into years.

Someone You Love

Someone you love

is lost and double-crossed tonight.

Someone you love is

in need of your direction.

Someone you love is in need of your strength and direction.

Someone you love is blind to your ways

and in need of your direction.

So whatever is

before me to do,

it is all there is to do today.

No matter what, it doesn't matter how,

someone you love is where he is supposed to be.

Someone you love is trusting

more and more,

believing in your power forever more.

We Are All in the Same Boat Now

We came on different ships

from different lands,

but we are all in the same boat now.

We once faced barriers and laws that kept us down,

but we are all in the same boat now.

We marched to Selma,

beaten to the ground,

but we are all in the same boat now.

We lived in a different world

across the tracks—

different values, different laws, different shacks—

but we are all in the same boat now.

Every now and again the same movement forms to take us back,

but the tree is rooted deep, and it is too far to turn back.

We are all in the same boat now.

So come together and face the pain;

come in closer out of the rain.

We are all in the same boat now.

In His Loving Arms

I woke up in gratitude today,

and it occurred to me

that all the things I thought

I needed and never got

were not a punishment assigned to me.

It was you holding me in your loving arms,

and when I wanted to get the thrill of serving myself,

you had better plans for me.

It was you holding me

in your loving arms.

So I had to learn gratitude

and appreciate your love for me

as you held me in your loving arms.

Sunday Blues

Sunday is the day I most

feel the blues.

All that is wrong comes up

like cream to the top.

I can't block, and I can't stop

these Sunday blues.

I have to deal with

what I feel.

I can't run and hide

from these blues of mine.

I wish that I could live another life,

the one I imagine that is free from strife,

but that would be a lie,

and then I would die.

I have to deal with this life of mine.

No matter what I feel,

I can't run and hide.

Nice and Easy

Nice and easy is the way

we love—

sweet like a baby, hands in a glove.

Come with me; let me show you how

nice and easy is the way we love,

like a baby in his mother's arms.

Come with me; let me show you how.

I see that darkness in your eyes.

I can tell that you are not connecting,

it is no surprise.

Lord knows you have tried.

Just when you break

and give up trying,

the light comes on to show you how.

So Far from Love Today

So far from love today,

I feel the pain and

know that it is I to blame.

So far from love today,

it is easy to forget when you are into you,

and then again,

it is so much of nothing,

and all of what nothing takes you through is

far from love today.

What is there to do when the deed is

done, and you come to understand

how come

you are so far from love today.

One Way or Another

One way or another

we are on our way.

One way or another

the light is here to stay.

So let's sleep in the spirit of love

tonight and see what the morning brings.

We might feel good enough to believe in

the spirit of love some more.

One way or another

we are on our way.

The dark days are gone,

the light is here to stay.

We have seen the darkest hour,

we have had the blues and the burning fire.

Just when we were about to give up

the spirit came and picked us up.

Calliaqua Town

When I was a boy

in Calliaqua town,

I would roam with my friends

Bookseta and Big Jim all day long.

Calliaqua town, Calliaqua town,

I hear you calling me when I am down.

Every day I was wandering

around, playing, fishing, swimming,

or getting lost in my little town.

Calliaqua, oh Calliaqua,

I hear you calling me when

things are rough.

I see visions of the days when

playing with friends,

no matter what, no matter where.

Visions of these days always serve to keep me safe.

If I Had the Wings of a Dove

Adaptation from Psalm 55:6–10

If I had the wings of a dove,

I would fly away and find me rest.

Lord, I would wander far off

and remain in the wilderness.

I would hasten my escape

from the storm, violence, and strife

in the cities.

Day and night the people go about

their mischief.

There is so much sorrow in the

midst of it.

If I had the wings of a dove,

I would fly away,

and I would find me rest.

Exiled in Pooler

Exiled in Pooler,

a long way from home,

constantly moving and feeling alone.

Looking and yearning, hoping

to find that place in the picture in my mind.

I am exiled in Pooler; it seems

like I am going to lose that place, and

it may be too late to find.

What if there is a question of fate that I am right where I belong?

Well, exiled in Pooler, like or not,

there is no need to search.

I am already where I belong.

Exiled in Pooler, it's where I belong now.

I am not going back to the island, man.

I have traded white sand for red clay,

the ocean for a pond.

Exiled in Pooler where I belong,

I have traded white sand for red clay,

but I am still an island man.

Freight Train

Every morning round about three,

I am lying here again on my back,

only to hear that lonely sound

of a freight train going through

Pooler town.

Wherever they go, it won't be long

before I hear that lonesome sound.

Oh! Freight train going through Pooler town.

Freight train, freight train moving through this town,

wake me up again with that lonesome sound—

freight train moving through this town.

Oh! That old lonesome sound.

Red Rock

Red Rock Ginger Ale

since 1885,

with just the right taste.

Red Rock Ginger Ale since 1885,

with just the right taste.

I have never had Red Rock

when I didn't sneeze, have a runny nose, and cough my lungs out.

Red Rock made a believer out of me.

It is true, Red Rock is sure to make you blow your nose and sneeze.

It's a power like

no other I have tasted before.

In the end, Red Rock gets the job done.

You know I am a believer despite a sneeze or two.

I still can't resist its might.

They say Red Rock—it is just the right taste for me.

A Slight Return

Here I would like to introduce some of my brother's artwork. My brother Franklyn was a mere thirty-seven years old when he left this life in 1990. Twenty-three years later, I miss him every day. However, he left me a wonderful legacy.

Franklyn was an artist. He found himself at a very young age, and he never looked back; no matter the consequences, he blazed the trail. Franklyn lived life with a passion. He was forever focused and determined. One piece of his legacy that he left me is a collection of art that I have surrounded myself with.

On his deathbed he said, referring to his art, "Take care of my babies." I have pieces of his work all around my office. In some ways, it is like having his energy here with me all of the time. There is not a day in this office when I am not viewing, reflecting, wondering, and talking to him silently. He gives me energy and a sense of majesty and love.

I truly believe that it is time to share this side of Franklyn with my community and the world. Franklyn remains on the mystical side—or as Van Morrison sings, "Into the Mystic." He was the first to see the wonder in the things before him. He never backed down, and I love him for that. He transcended time and space. It becomes quite obvious in viewing his art that he had a very uncommon approach to things. He always was able to look at life and art in a different way. Here are some examples of his work.

57

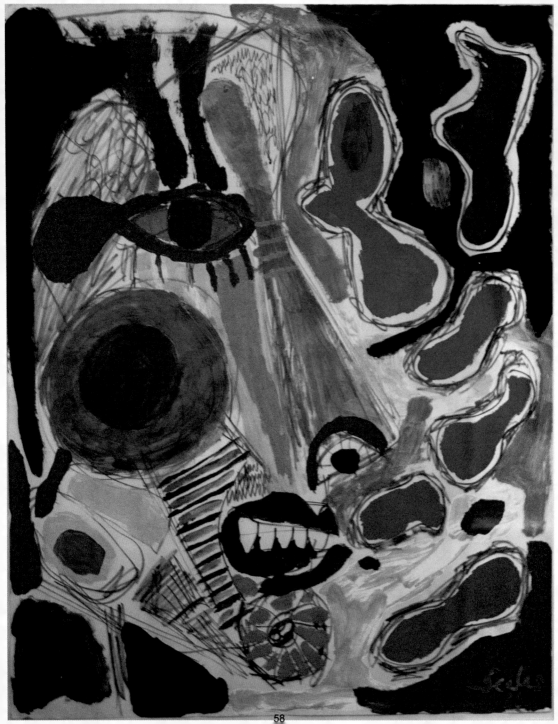

ABOUT THE AUTHOR

Dr. Lennox G. Seales is a psychotherapist working in Pooler, Georgia. He has worked as a therapist for the past thirty-two years in the Savannah area. Seales specializes in the treatment of chemically dependent clients. This is his second book; his first, *Praying the Blues*, was published in 2007.

In addition to writing, Seales is a guitarist and songwriter. He holds a doctorate from Westbrook University and a masters from Georgia Southern University. He was born on the Eastern Caribbean Island of Saint Vincent and immigrated to the United States as a teenager. He completed high school and college in New York.

Seales lives with his wife, Juanita, in Pooler, Georgia. They have three grown children and a grandson.

ABOUT THE BOOK

The Broad Highway is an accessible guide to possibilities. Many times we drift into hopelessness, and we need a guide to hope. We have the power to redirect our lives with a firm commitment to live based on spiritual principles that results in new meaning and purpose. We can learn to let go of struggle and strife, and to connect to spirit. We could practice doing the opposite of everything that drove us to failure and regret. Come on the broad highway!

Printed in the United States
By Bookmasters